ode to stanley

ode to stanley

*ramblings, ditties and stories,
conceived of reality, born of love*

donna redmond brownell

Writers Club Press
San Jose New York Lincoln Shanghai

ode to stanley
rambling, ditties, and stories, conceived of reality, born of love

All Rights Reserved © 2000 by Donna Brownell

No part of this book may be reproduced or transmitted in any form or by any means, graphic, electronic, or mechanical, including photocopying, recording, taping, or by any information storage retrieval system, without the permission in writing from the publisher.

Writers Club Press
an imprint of iUniverse.com, Inc.

For information address:
iUniverse.com, Inc.
5220 S 16th, Ste. 200
Lincoln, NE 68512
www.iuniverse.com

ISBN: 0-595-13605-2

Printed in the United States of America

This book is dedicated to everyone in my family…I love you all! To my friends, old and new and to all that have touched my life in some way, giving me a true appreciation for what is important. Thank you.

Epigraph

A wise man once said, "and this too shall pass".
Thank you Dad.

Contents

Preface xi

Acknowledgements xiii

Family Poems 1
    oh brother 3
    the note 4
    a darling child, pure and true 6
    fourth grade camping trip… 7
    Trilogy of Poems 9
    happy 25th anniversary 11
    thoughts of family 13
    daddy (oh Father) 14

Deep Thoughts 15
    dreams 17
    the wonder that i feel 18
    warm feeling 19
    loneliness 20
    memories 22
    the closeness i feel 24
    silent mentor 25
    a look back in time 26
    my secret 27

Loss 29
    broken link 31
    tears 32
    see 33
    my loss 35

Myself 37
   butterfly 39
   me 40

Life 41
   life's path 43
   life as i know it 44
   life 45

Friendship 47
   call on me… 49
   the lady in the green clog shoes…. 50
   friendship 52

Natures Beauty 55
   lilacs, daffodil and rose..57
   iris, crocus 58
   daisies 59
   my garden 60
   autumn trees 62
   fall days 63
   spring is here…finally 64

Love 67
   possession of a love divine 69
   a measure of love 70

Hodgepodge 71
   teddy bears 73
   no talent 74
   washington, d.c. 76
   morning whispers 77
   dragons and kings… 78

Seasonal 79
   seasonal friends 81
   end of year blues 82
   christmas-time without you 83

Preface

I have always written poems…from the time I was in late elementary school. I always thought I had something important to say; though Lord only knows why. I used to think it was fun to come up with lots of different ways of saying the same thing. I try to put the lessons I have learned in life into words. I have been blessed with many circumstances in my life that has made me appreciate many others, and for this I am grateful. I hope while reading this book you get some feeling for what I am trying to express. I hope these ramblings ditties and stories will have some impact on your life. Please enjoy.

Acknowledgements

With deep gratitude to my family, whose love and strength have forged a will of steel, a desire to make change and hope, for a better tomorrow.

To my many friends old and new, who have touched my life for a moment or a lifetime, thank you.

Last but not least, I would like to thank my new friends, Kim and Kenneth Moore. Kim, for her hospitality, instant friendship, kindness and the editing of this book, thank you. Kenneth for his unwavering encouragement, help in putting this book together from start to finish, and his un-ending support. This book truly became a reality because of them. Thanks!

Family Poems

oh brother

oh brother, i can't believe you can be such a pain
oh brother, i can't believe we're sharing puddles made of rain.
oh brother, i am mad at you for all the things you do
you pester me, you bother me, but that is just so you.
you are ornery and playful and bounding with energy
you make me feel slow and girlish; i don't want your company.
when we climb or run or ride, you're faster
when we play army, you get shots i cannot master.
you make everyone laugh and reel
it always seemed like you got the deal.
you there, blonde and smiling and round
climbing a tree, rolling on the ground.
the teacher would punish you quicker than heck,
but you'd say she was a pain in the neck.
then along you came one day, early from school
the teacher said to the girls you were cruel.
you became ill that day, never to know life like that again
you soon knew only heartache and pain.
then through the years, though there were many good times,
you had many serious up hill climbs.
now once again, it appears another milestone has come to you
i would take it upon myself if it was something i could do.
but you will, as usual, take it in stride
you'll catch the next bus and take the full ride.

the note

a day in june, just last year
a note from you arrived
it said that you'd be coming soon
our hope had been revived.

we thought and laughed and cried a lot,
the joy was sheer delight,
we dreamed about the time we'd meet
on delivery night.

we took a special class at night,
meant only for the two
who were picked by God to be the ones
to love and welcome you.

we carefully selected,
a middle-man to be
there to help us with your entrance,
into society.

then a little while later,
once all the plans were laid,
we thanked the Lord and waited
for the miracle we made.

the special moment happened,
and not to our surprise

you were born a beautiful, darling girl
with wondrous ice blue eyes.

and when they laid you next to me,
we thought our hearts would burst,
this was the moment we waited for,
born to us, our first.

from that time on, our love has grown,
a bond has strengthened too,
for every moment you've been with us,
our hearts have beat for you.

a darling child, pure and true

alone i sit and think of you
a darling child, pure and true.
a precious sign of life to me
a symbol of love arranged for three.
a part you are of Mom and Dad,
a symbol of the love we've had.
a kiss upon your button nose
we love you from your head to toes.
we smile at you every minute
we have no thought without you in it.
each day we make all kinds of plans
we hope you know you are in good hands.
hands that will guide you through life's pain
and the misty moments that come with the rain.
we'll stay beside you through night and day,
and be there to comfort you in every way.
we'll hold your hands and kiss your tears
and love you forever, God bless the years.
we'll be your friends in times of need
there will be times like that indeed.
alone i sit and think of you
a darling child, pure and true.

fourth grade camping trip...

try to have a good time
a time to cherish so
a time to feel free and happy
and let your feelings flow.

don't think about your home life
your mommy or your dad
just think about the fun times
and experiences you've had.

remember to be good and safe
do **not** what's wrong, but right
then think of those who love you
when you close your eyes at night.

if as you lay there resting
your thoughts turn to those you love
remember that we're thoughtful too
of **our** gift from above.

you are our special angel
and incase you didn't know
it bothered **us** more to allow you
than it bothered **you** to go.

but you're growing up so quickly
and a lady you'll soon be
and as you look back on your life
you'll think this was fun…you'll see!!
Love always mommy

Trilogy of Poems

i wish that i had said it more
a thousand times may do
instead of only three or four
the word, "i love you!"

as all things have a reason
as all things have a rhyme
all things have a season
and all things have a time.

Danny
beautiful, wanted, smiling
protective, loud, friendly, argumentative, helpful,
peaceful, reflective, alone,
gone.

dear michael,

thank you for the things you say
when i am feeling low
thank you for being there
when i need somewhere to go.
thank you for the confidence
you instill deep in my being
thank you for the calming hand
when my sanity is fleeing.
thank you for the memories
you give, that i hold dear
and thank you for the times that you
have held me, oh so near.
thank you for the moments
i'm left breathless from your love
thank you for the tenderness
i dream so often of.
thank you for the lift you give
when loneliness is mine
and thank you for the honesty,
i can count on all the time.
and thank you for the thrill you bring
to every breath i take,
thank you for the kindness
and for the love we make.
i'd like to say to you,
thank you the most for holding me,
and letting me hold you.

happy 25th anniversary
love now and forever…donna

happy 25th anniversary

mike,

it's been twenty-five years, so squint your eyes and see,
that fine figure of a woman, i used to be.
before my belly and my breasts hung low,
before my memory lapsed and my gait got slow.
before my muscle tone all turned to flab,
when my butt weighed *less* than a cement slab.
when my breasts were high and firm and round
before my body gained these pounds.
when vain was something good to be
not lines protruding below my knees. (veins)
before stretch marks came from babies,
when promises were *yes* and not just *maybes*.
when my hair was long and thick and brown
and all this gray wasn't hanging around.
when my eyes were deep and clear and could see
before braille classes were being formed for me.
when my hands were strong and my grip like a vise
when my skin wasn't wrinkled and my body was nice.
back when my feet weren't gnarled from use and abuse
when i could turn a man's head who wasn't mr. tenuse.
when i could stay up all night and not snore when i slept
when i could drink all night and up the stairs i still crept.
when my lipstick stayed put, didn't run into grooves,
when i had to be careful, 'cause guys put on the moves.

when "night time" meant "bedtime" and "bedtime" meant "sleep"
before my emotions would drop me in a heap.
before my aches and my pains could get the best of me,
before my mustache was darker than the guy's down the street.
before my glasses were permanently tied 'round my neck,
when my children would listen when i gave them heck.
before post-it notes were something that i bought galore,
back when i remembered what i needed when i went to the store.
when i simply just did it, didn't have to motivate
when i was too busy to be on time, so i was late.
before my life turned into hours of lonesome time
when i kept the kids busy and free from grime.
when i think back to the times that i thought were so lame
i have to admit now, it was youth i should blame.

love always, donna

thoughts of family

…and i said to my friend, "why do you say that?" she says, "oh, i don't know, it just seems that family is more trouble than it is worth sometimes. like around the holidays…seems like a lot of bother to me. i can't imagine that your family is really so close. it doesn't seem normal to me." i frown, not even coming close to understanding her statement and say, "i don't think it is abnormal at all. i think it is as it should be." she returns, "well, maybe, but how can you do it, especially with so many? how can you worry about so many and not go crazy?" i laugh and say, "well, i never said we weren't crazy, only that we care for each other, respect each other and love each other. we are there for each other. maybe because there are so many of us, we have had plenty of practice and it is just second nature now, i don't know." she rolls her eyes, not understanding in the slightest what i just said. i rise from the chair and on my way across the room, i smile with a surely contented smile and silently mouth the words, "thanks mom and dad, i am proud of my family."

daddy (oh Father)

i am sorry for all that i have done wrong
you raised me to be righteous, moral and strong.
you raised me to be certain of everything I do,
yet even with you raising me, i'm not as good as you.
you taught us all the gift of love,
to embrace the people we think of.
you taught us to be quick and bright
to gravitate toward a positive light.
you told us so many things, i'll never re-call
i wish i had recorded it all.
the cliques, ditties, proverbs and sayings
were as important to me, as all the praying.
they comfort me, even to this day
a great Father you were in every way.
you called me your social butterfly
do you know you are the reason why?
you were my glowing social example
you taught me life was to be sampled.
i did, i have and i'm glad i'm me
though most others cannot see.
why or how, i'm like this
may as well just add it to the list,
of things that make me different, odd
but you know, we were peas of the same pod.
that is why i miss you so much more
than anyone i've lost before.

Deep Thoughts

dreams

i've been touched by angels, and have touched some back
i've stood in perils path
i've tasted life's bitter pills
and drank from the fountain of love.

i've kissed the blarney stone of laughter
i swam in oceans of despair
i've climbed the mountains of trauma
and i've listened with baited breath to the song of hope.

i've touched with tender fingertips, loveliness
i've encountered fearful times
i've lifted spirits and shattered myths
i've felt loneliness with a heavy heart.

i've never lived a moment not important
i've never forgotten a dream come true
i've never lost faith in humanity
i've gained strength through my weaknesses.

the wonder that i feel

the wonder that i feel is a strong comfort to me at times when my world has taken leave of it's senses. it is a feeling of being lucky that life goes on as i know it, no matter what life throws at me. now, i know there are limits to what anyone can handle and i hope i do not reach mine, but am confident in the realization of what i have been able to handle in my life to this point.

please God, my ever-present wish is that you not test me beyond my limit. i knowthis is not a fair request for we all must bear our quota of crosses, as i will too, but don't let me take that one last step that will thrust me into the world of terror that is beyond my limit.

thank you God for all the obstacles you have arranged for me to overcome, without losing sight of what i had to achieve. i am thankful for each and every one of them. they have kept me strong and taught me lessons i may not otherwise have learned. i know the me i have become is a gift, and i cherish it, because it came from you.

warm feeling

i have the warmest feeling
so deep within my soul,
it sets my heart to thumpin'
makes my stomach roll.

it kinda makes me wonder
it makes me stop and sigh,
it makes me sooo darn happy
i don't even wonder why.

it makes me sit back some
and settle for a while,
it's one of those special things
that makes you want to smile.

i can't name it or describe it
I can barely tell you how…
it comes to be with me
only that it's with me now.

so each time you feel it, grab it
just don't let it go
you'll know it when you feel it,
so, let the good stuff show.

loneliness

loneliness is setting in
and darkness grips the day
i have some feelings deep inside
but don't know what to say.

i tell someone of my deepest pain
and try to make them see
how much i am crying inside
how i've lost a part of me.

i've said good-bye to folks i love
and know that i never again will feel
the closeness i've enjoyed to date
the love i know that is so real.

to kiss their spirit one last time
and wave with open hand
to know i'll never feel their touch
gone the lives we've planned.

a prayer of condolence
i guess you'd say for me
one last wish for my friends
a silent, hopeful plea.

and as i hope with all my heart
to my God above
i pray Paradise is near
for the ones i love.

memories

collecting all my memories, to store them deep in my soul
to take out and share with those i love
dare i be so bold?

some feel it's best to bury death
and accept it, for it's true
but i have got my own way
to keep from feeling blue.

i line up all my memories
and hold them to my heart
i carefully re-live them
so we will never be apart.

i laugh at what was funny
and cry again for the pain
and make sure they are neatly tucked
back in my heart again.

at times when i am lonely,
i conjure up the good old days
and ever so gently i touch them,
they're clear though covered with haze.

i can tell by the feeling of peace i have,
that this plan is right for me.
it brings me the quiet that i need
and lets me see what most cannot see.

the closeness i feel

a moment spent with people known,
can cost a thousand tears,
and a moment spent with strangers though,
can seldom quench life's fears.
so how could this have happened, that a
stranger you have never been,
from the moment i met you, my heart just
let you in.
so few can understand this feeling, so
few will ever own it,
but you are one of the chosen few, so if
you'd like; i'll loan it.

silent mentor

he walks slowly, while going against a howling wind
there's a sadness about him that I speak of only to myself.
hat on head; cane in hand, he stops to look around
nothing familiar, a tear appears in the corner of his eye.
i wait and watch. he'll be fine once again, i assure myself.
he then turns and walks toward me, a slight wave of the hand,
i turn to go, but am compelled to see what he needs.
i walk toward the gentle, old stranger with a soft pity in my heart,
he extends a hand, i accept it, and slowly my pity disappears.
he smiles a handsome, though tired smile and tells me he's glad to finally meet me.
he gives me his name and i tell him mine, as well.
a curious thing happened at that moment
i felt the strange sensation of seeing myself many years down the road
alone, perhaps facing my own mortality, but not ceasing to want love and companionship.
as i took my hand back, i felt the need to touch this kind soul again,
so i reached out to place a gentle hand on his arm and he responded quickly with a smile.
i asked him if he enjoyed his walk. he said; "oh yes, very much," and i smiled.
he asked me if i enjoyed my walk and i frowned, as it had been a while since i had.
he slowly moved in a circle to take in nature's backdrop,
and with his cane, he waved to the world and said, "what's **not** to enjoy? life is so **beautiful**."

a look back in time

as i look back, i see that the days of black and white, had to be,
for without the absolutes we would never learn of the maybes.
without the maybes we would never learn of the possibilities,
without the possibilities, we would never learn of the dreams.
without the dreams,
we would never live.

my secret

i have a little secret, that hardly anyone knows
i've always kept this secret, and never let it show.
i may have mentioned something 'bout it,
i really don't know…

i hold this secret holy, it's only meant for me
it's something i feel good about, it's peaceful as can be
but sometimes i will leave a hint,
just so others see…

i wish that someone else could feel it
though i don't want anyone to steal it
i think it's meant for only me,
but still, i want to reveal it…

i wonder if others would understand
if i took them by the hand
and actually let them know,
what makes me take this stand…

well, i'll take the chance and i will tell
but you may not understand…oh well
maybe at one point you will
and life's fears, i may quell…

it's just a matter of how i think
in textures soft and shades of pink
not everyone does this i know,
some feel it rough, i feel it mink...

so take these words and try to see
the secret held inside of me
i hope you guess it, yeah i do,
then peaceful you will always be...

Loss

broken link

we were a circle
made of a chain
a link is gone
but the rest remain.

it is now open
it may never close
though we all try
heaven knows.

our strength has faded
we're not so tough
we try to be
but it's not enough.

we go through the motions
it's necessary for us to
but **always** there are
lingering thoughts of you.

if it gets better
and I hope it can
we'll never forget
we want peace for us all, Dan.

tears

i've always been a crier
tears always flowed with ease
my heart was always bruised
but at least i **did** know peace.

it never took an earthquake
to move me to a sob
a small dose of melancholy
was sure to do the job.

i've always had to pull for
the underdog it seems
the confident and winners
seemed to have their own means.

i never knew what pain was, though
until you went away
and hope that i will feel some peace
before **my** dying day.

see

look into **my** eyes
though full, they may appear
they're empty signs, reminders
of love, loss by death, of fear.

look into **my** soul
a loneliness so real
you may not understand
the oneness that **i** feel.

look into **my** mind
memories of times past
i have to hold onto every one
a lifetime, **they** must last.

look into **my** life
it's different than it had been
before **you** went away
i wish **i** had known when.

because then…

i would have looked into **your** eyes
and seen how empty they appeared
they were signs, i missed
of all the things **you** feared.

i'd have looked into **your** soul
your loneliness i'd feel
i should have understood
that **all** of it was real.

i'd have looked into **your** heart
and prayed for it to keep you…
going long enough
for us to help **you** get through.

i'd have looked into **your** mind
and taken away the pain
and given hope to help **you**
to the sunshine, from the rain.

and i 'd have looked into **your** life
and have hoped that **you** could see
how it would be now
for the rest of them and me.

my loss

what have i learned
since you checked out?
i've learned some things
like…what life is about.

i've learned to think
past the moment and
to give a hug
to hold a hand.

to listen to
the voice of pain
to hide my tears
behind the rain.

to share my feelings
with those who care
there are a lot
of them out there.

i've learned sometimes
you have to let it out
and that love is
what it's all about.

Myself

butterfly

sometimes i wish i could curl myself into a tight little cocoon, where i could keep myself warm and safe until i had time to observe the world around me. i'd keep a small portion of myself to take out when i had the confidence to show it to others. i'd make sure they would love that part of me that was purely me, before i let it show. i'd nurture and love it to show, by example, how i want them to love it too. i'd make it a point of protecting for the sake of myself, that small unique bit of me, that i would want everyone to love and accept. oh, but there are warnings that come with this desire. i would warn myself, "be strong, be right, be good. they may not like you, but do not compromise your integrity, do not weaken, for the gratuitous love of others, for you will lower the standards for the rest of the world, if you do so and are accepted." i would tell that small scared part of myself to strike out, to chance the unlikely, for with chance and success, comes respect, the one thing you really want in life.

i'd put my arms around and stroke that small quiet part of me which no one knows, and tell it that if someone **did** know it, they would be envious of such a strong and noble character. they would strive to emulate this character in a way that people from the same region tend to speak alike. i'd mention how they would cheer you for the way you held out to show that even though you have chosen the lonely, different and sometimes un-fun path, you chose the path that brought you to the point in your life where you are in love with yourself and do so respect yourself. this point in your life is what everyone works toward. some reach it sooner than others; some will not really try. but now that you have, i will unfurl the cocoon that has protected you, my spirit, and release you, so that you might show by example what taking the road less traveled might bring. then you will see, as a mature butterfly, you will experience the freedom of growth.

me

i'm silly, i'm pensive, i worship the act,
i'm profound, i'm clip and i love to yak.
i'm lonely, i'm cheery and oh so abrupt
i'm a loser, a winner, i never give up.
i have experienced pain and privilege is mine
i am hurrying along, but i've got lots of time.
i'm hard pressed for passion, regarding certain ordeals,
yet i'm a force to be reckoned with, about how i feel.
i have stood on principal, till my knees have given in
i have argued a point, then turned easy as sin.
i have noted with respect, my shortcomings and my long,
i have noticed each new day, something i have done wrong.
i have been amazed at what i miss when i look,
and i have to take credit for some chances i took.
i seldom miss a trick, unless it stares me in the face,
i hardly ever stumble over things left out of place.
but take away the obvious and just try to trick me then,
i'm quick, i'm sharp and i'll tell you when…
and where and how and why and you'll understand,
why some of me is mediocre and some of me is grand.
but no matter what you know, or how you think it be,
one thing is for sure…you can depend on me.

Life

life's path

life's experience, where does it end?
with deep conversations shared with good friends.
an evening of trying to fit it all in
by taking your life out of folders and bins.

you announce every detail and share every pain
and when you finish these topics, you share them again.
you laugh softly and whisper certain details
you may hoot and holler, but it never fails,

you always will tell a friend of your woe,
it's like there is no other place for you to go.
we bolster each other in ways we don't see
and when we leave them, our heart is light and free.

as i sit back and think of what i miss in my life
it's time with my friends, not less toil and strife.
some people feel lucky, with less problems and pain
but give me my friends and the rest can remain.

i'll get through the tough times, the hard times i swear,
as long as i know my friends will be there.

life as i know it

i consider my life as i know it and i am proud of its twists and turns. no one really knows where it will go, we only hope that the destination is as colorful as the trip itself. so often we are on a smooth and slow route, only to be jousted off the road of easy to find we are on a bumpy, somewhat difficult thoroughfare, and it is at this time we realize we are most alive. this is not a coincidence; it is the effort we must put into making the trip, that actually makes the trip a pleasure. and as we exert ourselves in a more conscious way, we see clearly what we have been missing as we trodded along the clear and narrow path. it is not always a burden. it is often a gift. it can be a momentous time when we can see ourselves better than others see us. this is not always easy, but when we truly open our eyes and see who and what we are, who and what we have become, it is immediately apparent that we can either remain the person we are or simply change. the older one gets, the more possible this seems, the easier to achieve. but no less important. all of us, must re-evaluate our lives in time with our changing destiny. it may seem as though this is difficult to do, but by opening ourselves up to others, we open up to ourselves too.

i so appreciate the changes i have made in myself and quite possibly inspite of myself. i know that as i crawl, walk or run through life the only thing i can be sure of is that life will change, and for this i am grateful, for without it we would be in awe of the world around us and in fear of our reaction to it.

life

a moment, one, like any other
can change a life beyond compare
and make you wonder why you bother
can take hearts here and give heart there.

a fleeting moment, marked in time
can surely seem forever
can make time stop, or make time fly
or seem it didn't happen…ever.

i tackle time as most folks do
i try to make the good times last
i try to push away the few
times…i hate, from the past.

i truly think that all time counts
as surely does the outcome
of any pressure that does mount
and this can make us numb.

Friendship

call on me...

if you do get lonely and you will, call on me.
if you wake up crying and you will, call on me.
if you cannot think clearly, call on me.
if you feel an overwhelming load on your shoulders,
and you will, call on me.

for i will fill your time with friendship,
i will try my best to ease your sorrow,
i will try to help you see things clearer,
and i will carry the load, so you might rest, if you call on me.

the lady in the green clog shoes....

there is a woman that i met
she is unique as she can be
she has loads of love for all mankind
and the animal kingdom indeed.

she will go on for hours about the pets
she keeps and how she raised them,
she'll tell you of how with them she slept
while she disciplined and praised them.

her house is full of loving things
momentos of bygone days
pictures and paintings of colors and
some in blacks, whites and grays.

she's creative and whimsical and
serious when she needs to be,
talk to her and you will find
a class act from a to z.

she has traveled a lot, which only adds
to her worldly and unique persona
she's overcome adversity and pain
they can't get her down, they're not gonna.

she surrounds herself with good things
with family and friends of old
she's well settled in to her life
she's the leader of a comfortable fold.

so continue she will, to enrich the world
with her bouncy personality and charm,
she's the keeper of the helpless,
she's the warder off of harm.

she's the kind of person,
whom you would say of
"i'm awfully glad i met her,
she's a treasure from God above."

friendship

what your friendship means to me?
it's better than a happy tree.
it's soft and fluffy, clean and nice
let's repeat it once or twice.

it's cozy, warm and such a delight,
i'm thankful for it day and night.
it's sleek and shiny…all the more,
reason that i keep it for.

i hold it to my heart and pray
it will be with me everyday.
i lay it 'fore my eyes to see
do you know just what it means to me?

it makes me want to live each day
in the very nicest way.
it makes me strive to do my best
before i allow myself to rest.

it gives me meaning in a world of doubt,
it makes me strong when i am out.
it let's me sort the good from bad,
it points out to me, the fun i've had.

it makes life's little mysteries clear,
it makes the strange, not sooo queer.
it helps to know that you are there
and when you're not, i still know where.

it makes for happy, well-lived minutes
so many a thought have you in it.
i'm thankful to my lord above,
for this special kind of love.

so if you think of me today
know i'll think of you that way.
and if i do not call your name,
know i thought of you just the same.

Natures Beauty

lilacs

the color is impressive
the aroma is so fine
the clarity is wonderful
the whole darn thing's divine.

daffodil

six points like the star of david
a bell that has no chime
a beautiful burst of yellow
a lovely, silent rhyme.

rose

a rose is as pretty a flower
as a flower could ever be
you could stare at a rose for hours
but your heart will never be free.

iris

a shade more purple than night-time
a scent to enamor her man
the iris is loving and beautiful
goes as gently as any lover can.

crocus

push back the snow
along the gate
don't miss it now
crocuses won't wait!

daisies

the daisy is a friend of mine
they grow in fields, not in a line
i lay in fields of tall grass and clover
and thought of daisies, over and over.
i've plucked the petals from their stalks
as i said, "love poems" on my walks
i've rolled in daisies and laughed with glee
while others wondered what was wrong with me.
so, pick a daisy and hold it near
for daisies are more than flowers dear.

my garden

i spend time in my garden
i do enjoy it so
my flowers are all around me
as long as there's no snow.
i fasten *bachelor buttons*
on a coat of silk
i have *tulips* to open
so I can drink my milk.
i've tamed a *dandelion*
with the scent of lily and…
i've tried to plant a *sunflower*
unsuccessfully in the sand.
rose is a real *tomato*
and is happy as a lark
until her *morning glories* wouldn't bloom
especially in the dark.
i never *aster* 'bout it
if they blossomed in the morn
but *iris*, she informed me
she likes to keep herself warm.
my *baby's breath* is ever sweet
and stays so close to *mum*
the *daffodils* are sunny bright
and hope that you will come…
and see my garden and my friends

the one-stemmed kind i mean
i nurture and I care for them
with two thumbs that are green.

autumn trees

i wonder as i look at you
covered by the morning dew.
laden with leaves…such a load
i hope they'll stay…but it's turning cold.
and when the sun comes up and dries
the dew…and glares our tired eyes.
i try to drink in all the beauty,
because soon the leaves will have a duty.
they'll lie upon the base and keep
the moisture, seeds and magic deep.
so though they die, they soon will bring,
life back to that tree again…in spring.

fall days

leaves are swirling, round and round
they blow up, then hit the ground.
reds and yellows, greens and browns,
piled high in colored mounds.
such a crackling sound and rustle,
while through them school kids run and bustle.
the leaves all scurry down the street
and land on lawns that once were neat.
and oh, the time we spend to rake them,
then off to the fire-pile we take them.
no wonder we so enjoy it all—-
the beautiful, precious joys of fall.

spring is here…finally

the snow is melting quickly,
the mud is all around,
the sun is shining brightly
some crocuses were found.

the birds are fairly chirping
and the grass is really green
the pets are laying in the sun
temps are warmer than we've seen.

the geese are hanging by the pond
as turkeys gobble on the ridge,
the swans are swimming on the water,
walkers gather on the bridge.

the scenes of spring are hopeful
they can set your spirit right
they bring your interest out the door
keep you going, morning 'til night.

i feel my horizons broaden
as my thoughts turn to spring, indeed
i have taken on new hobbies
and that is just what i need.

for by the time that summer lands here
in about a week or two
i'll have forgotten what my plans are
summer making them too hard to do.

Love

possession of a love divine

what if we could possess
a love so divine that it takes our breath away?
a love so intense we can barely believe
that that love has found us today?

what if what we now feel has changed a hundred percent
and has made us believe we are great
what would be said of love then, to the whole human race
would more people believe in fate?

what if in the course of a day, not a lifetime
we could change our thinking to be
able to feel all the love we can hold
would this not make us feel free?

could we then just simply give back love
to the holders of strife and pain
and the people who fear dependency
to those suffering from stress and strain?

well, i think in my small world, i've found this
hidden away from the everyday pace
and i think as i strive to replace doubt
that i just may win the race.

a measure of love

do you measure your love in a beaker,
a cup, pint, liter or quart,
do you measure your love in a gallon
or do you measure your love in the heart?

can you measure your love with inches,
centimeters, feet, yards or miles
do you know that you've found this true love
by kilometers, meters or smiles?

i think all would agree when they find it
that not an acre or township or state
but a heart full of love, felt deeply and true
would make all of us feel great.

Hodgepodge

teddy bears

teddy bears are everywhere
on a shelf or in a nook
they're sitting on a rocking chair
or hanging on a hook.

they nestle on a pillowcase
or sit upon a sill
they receive so many hugs
i'm sure they always will.

sometimes you see them in a car
or huddled on a chair
they are so very comforting
they never pull your hair.

they come in many colors
and sizes…large and small
they never take what isn't theirs
teddy bears give all.

so if you're lonely and need a hug
a teddy bear will do
they give love unconditionally
and will always comfort you.

no talent

a musical life, we've all been raised on,
though none can play a beat
we can sing our little hearts out
but a single note we can't create.

we had song and dance at our house
and boy we were so good
we could cut the rug and yodel
but never like we should.

we would listen to our parents
and turn our nose up indeed
but now, of course, to others dismay
we **all** can sing the lead.

we can sing about the county fair
and oklahoma, bali hai
we have walked the yellow brick road
and even seen monkeys fly.

honey bun is a friend of ours
we'll sing her praise on high
and singing in the rain with gene kelly
has never left us dry.

we would sing while washing dishes
though we never admitted it was fun

but we'd go on for hours
even after the dishes were done.

we'd sing with linda ronstadt
and we couldn't see the forest for the trees,
we'd mammy with al jolson
and do sammy jr. on our knees.

we would sing when we went running
through the woods to visit a friend
we would sing and dance in the side street
we could charleston to the end.

we'd watch Mom and Dad do the boogie
and the jitterbug was all the rage
until the sixties brought all the good stuff
and we wrote our own little page.

we'd do the monkey and the watusi
the jerk, the pony and the fish
we'd sing all the new tunes and love them
and we could all dance the twist.

but of course, the tunes that we loved
didn't have the power to endure
so they cast out the sixties like garbage
and with the seventies came more.

well, the moral, I'd like to explain here
is that while we could sing from july until june
we aren't going to make any money
because none of us can carry a tune.

washington, d.c.

i look around in heightened awe…..
at sights of which i never saw….
such beauty, bound by steel and crete
the sidewalks strong beneath my feet.
i wonder at the monuments, i could fairly burst with pride
walking down the streets, my mother, brother at my side.

the symbolism and history, so much to comprehend
i stare ahead with tears in my eyes, what is around the next bend?
such great treasures that we own here
the patriotism that is on loan here.
you need not give it back today,
take it with you, when you go away.
remember all that freedom gives us
hold on to it, so it does not leave us.

as i look skyward to see the stone
of washington monument all alone
and i seek "the wall" for lonely reasons
alive with beauty in this season.

morning whispers

whispered into sleepy ears
misty moments of silence gone
wondering what will come of the years,
the words, "i hope the world goes on."

i felt the day shine bright outdoors
the room was gleaming too
i wonder whose voice called to me,
danny, could it be you?

i bolted up and sat a spell
and nearly felt at ease
then something else effected me
will wonders never cease?

a soft warm glow surrounded me
i felt at peace and yet
i'm wondering was it someone known
or someone i have not met.

dragons and kings...

ages ago when life was hard
and people needed help to go on
dragons and kings and knights and things
were called on to get things done.

though bigger than life to the simple folk
like peasants and serfs and the like
along they would come when needed
to help with the biggest of fights.

when damsels would scream from injustice and fear
and children would hide and stay hid
the doers of good would come riding in
on their steeds, offering comfort, protection and bread.

so to the people of yore, when they needed to know
that they were safe from the doers of ill
in rode the good guys to take up the pain
and i think we look to them still.

as i sit here and think maybe chivalry's dead
i must think of the new doers of good
and realize anew that for all that men do
there are those whose respect has stood.

Seasonal

seasonal friends

greenery, greenery, everywhere
big red bows of velvet and lace
did i tell you how much i really care?
and that i'll miss seeing your face?

did i mention how a tree really tops off a season
and egg nog makes things seem really top rate
did i tell you that i don't need a reason
to give gifts or to celebrate?

and did i happen to clear up
that i went to have lunch with a friend.
who needed to be cheered up
and was better off than me in the end?

oh, i wanted to bring up just one thing more
for you know i've really gotta go
do you work year after year in this store?
i've come to enjoy your company so.

end of year blues

christmas time, days of cheer
it's time to end the long last year.
it's been a doosey, yes indeed
terror, mayhem, joy and greed.

mud slides, fires, quakes, caused fear
sad stories we don't want to hear
happy moments, fleeting, maybe
births and deaths of newborn babies.

floods and snow storms,
sleet, ice and hail,
thunder and lightning
and pleasure without fail.

wind storms and power outages,
heat waves and more
sand storms and beautiful days
and downed trees galore.

but it's all what we make it
that much is true
i can take it or leave it,
how about you?

christmas-time without you

i think of howling wind and cold
the snow upon my roof
i chill to think the temperature
will turn rain to ice, as proof.

i watch as all the cars slow down,
almost to a halt.
i hope everyone is safe tonight,
that the trucks have dropped their salt.

i watch the news and weather too
i hear their tales of gloom
i pray everyone is warm tonight,
as i am, in my living room.

i smell the cookies baking
and sense the christmas cheer
and everything is perfect,
except that you're not here.

i look at our christmas tree
covered with ornaments and lights
i wonder if you have a tree
christmas just doesn't seem right.

i wrap the gift and presents
for you and everyone
they're pretty as can be,
but it just isn't any fun.

i know you must be lonely
and a chill must surely be yours
i hope that your new friends are kind
and that you are indoors.

and as you rise so early
and start your dreaded day
i hope you find a reason to
feel happy, bright and gay.

and as your day turns into night
and you grow tired and weary
remember that we're thinking of you
hoping your day's not dreary.

so on Christmas day, as you are there
and we are here without you,
remember how we love you
and that we're thinking 'bout you.